Gallery Books
Editor: Peter Fallon

TALBOT'S BOX

Thomas Kilroy

TALBOT'S
BOX

Gallery Books

Talbot's Box
was first published
by The Gallery Press in 1979.
New edition 1997.

The Gallery Press
Loughcrew
Oldcastle
County Meath
Ireland

© Thomas Kilroy 1979, 1997

Thomas Kilroy has asserted his right to be
identified as the author of this Work.

ISBN 1 85235 198 5

All rights whatsoever in this play are strictly reserved. Requests
to reproduce the text in whole or in part should be addressed
to the publishers. Application for performance in any medium
must be made in advance, prior to commencement of rehearsals,
and for translation into any language, to Casarotto Ramsay Ltd.,
60 Wardour Street, London W1V 4ND.
   The Gallery Press acknowledges the financial assistance of An
Chomhairle Ealaíon/The Arts Council, Ireland, and the Arts
Council of Northern Ireland.

Author's Note

Matt Talbot, working-man and mystic, was born on 2 May 1856, the second of twelve children, in the savage poverty of the Dublin slums. He was an early victim of the alcoholism rampant among the poor of the city. At the age of twenty-eight he underwent a remarkable change and undertook the pledge of total abstinence from alcohol as part of the Catholic temperance movement. The change, however, had more to do with the secret life which he lived from this point until his death on 7 June 1925.

While still remaining an unskilled worker all his life, he followed a daily routine of severe physical penance, fasting and prayer. The full extent of this only became known after his death and a cult of Matt Talbot soon began, especially in the working-class areas of the city associated with his life. The movement towards his canonisation as a saint of the Roman Catholic Church began in 1931. Six years later a Papal Decree allowed him to be called Venerable, or Blessed, a 'Servant of God'. A bridge over the river Liffey, opened in 1978, has been called, with a peculiarly Dublin mixture of feelings, the Talbot Memorial Bridge.

Talbot lived through the crucial period of modern Irish history, the last decades of the nineteenth century, the Great Lock-out of Dublin workers in 1913, the rebellion of 1916 and the Independence of the new state. But none of this really impinged upon his life, with one exception. As a trade unionist, his part in the Great Lock-out is a matter of continuing dispute. There is a long-standing Dublin taunt of Matt Talbot the Scab, the betrayer of his fellow-workers. There is the counter-

defence by, among others, contemporary trade union-
ists, that Matt Talbot subscribed fully to the rights of the
workers.

I wanted to write a play about the mystic and the
essentially irreducible division between such extreme
individualism and the claim of relationship, of community, society. I was also interested in the way individuals
of exceptional personality invite manipulation and the
projection of the needs of others. There is a sense in
which Matt Talbot is but the occasion of this play in that
I believe that a figure like this transcends any one profes-
sion of belief. The kind of texture which the play has,
however, derives from the idiom of the Dublin streets.

In the beginning I was possessed by the crude
manipulation of an eccentric, inaccessible man by forces
which sought a model for the purpose of retaining
power over people. What I think I wrote was a play about
aloneness, its cost to the person, and the kind of courage
required to sustain it. I also wanted to write about death
in an entertaining way which would be, finally, life-
enhancing.

Talbot's Box was first produced in the Peacock Theatre, Dublin, on 13 October 1977, as part of the Dublin Theatre Festival, with the following cast:

MATT TALBOT	John Molloy
FIRST MAN	Stephen Brennan
SECOND MAN	Clive Geraghty
WOMAN	Ingrid Craigie
PRIEST FIGURE	Eileen Colgan

Director	Patrick Mason
Design	Wendy Shea
Lighting	Tony Wakefield

Note: The priest figure should be played by an actress.

in memory of my mother and father

ACT ONE

Before the lights go up, the strains of the hymn 'Faith of Our Fathers'
may be heard from a massed choir. The lights reveal a huge box
occupying virtually the whole stage, its front closed to the audience.
The effect should be that of a primitive, enclosed space, part prison,
part sanctuary, part acting space. As the hymn dies away, the front of
the box is opened out from within by two men so that the audience now
sees inside: three walls, perhaps with daubed signs and objects of a
religious shrine. All the actors, costumes and props required in the play
are already within the box. These latter include a mobile pedestal,
mobile pulpit and a mobile hospital trolley, whose glittering metal
contrasts with the prevailing timber of the box. The two men, in
blooded white medical coats take up positions beside the trolley which
is well upstage. On it is a human figure covered by a sheet. We find the
PRIEST FIGURE busily manipulating the pedestal into position to one
side. On it, statuesque, is the WOMAN, in the costume and pose of a
statue of the Virgin. Having arranged this statue satisfactorily, the
PRIEST FIGURE, in soutane and biretta, ascends the pulpit on the other
side of the stage and addresses the audience.

PRIEST FIGURE (*Benevolent*) My dear brethren in Jesus Christ! We
are gathered here this evening to give honour to
Matt Talbot (1856-1925). A simple Dublin working
man. For years he had been a drunkard. A sinner.
But then, my dear brethren, then — at the age of
twenty-eight he was touched by the Holy Spirit.
He reformed. Gave up the drink —

WOMAN (*Shout*) How long do I have to stand like this?

PRIEST FIGURE (*Aside*) Shush! You're supposed to be the statue of
the Blessed Virgin Mary!

WOMAN Don't I know it!

PRIEST FIGURE Silence! Show a little respect in the holy presence!

WOMAN OK, OK, OK.

PRIEST FIGURE (*Resuming*) Yes — Yes, my dear ah-brethren. At

9

twenty-eight Matt Talbot reformed. And for forty years — forty years — he lived a life of secret penance. Secret to all, that is, but Almighty God. Then on Trinity Sunday, 1925, he collapsed in Granby Lane in Dublin city. And when they came to take him, they discovered that he had bound himself with penitential chains, cords —

WOMAN I'm going to get a cramp if this goes on much longer!

PRIEST FIGURE (*Bravely*) Such penance — such prayer — like a strong light, you see, blazing, and then he passed from this valley of darkness into eternal light —

WOMAN (*Sniff*) There's a smell in here.

PRIEST FIGURE What, my dear brethren, does this mean to us?

WOMAN (*More loudly*) I said there's a smell in here!

PRIEST FIGURE A what?

WOMAN A smell. Y'know —

PRIEST FIGURE What do you mean, a smell?

WOMAN A bit like — perspiration —

PRIEST FIGURE Perspir-

WOMAN Body odour.

PRIEST FIGURE Body — hold on a moment — in the church! Retain your pious pose! (*Produces large aerosol can, jumps down from pulpit spraying all about intoning prayers in Latin*) There you are! (*Looks about in satisfaction*)

WOMAN It's only getting worse!

PRIEST FIGURE Remain on your pedestal at all costs! (*Further spraying about*)

WOMAN I will not! (*Jumps down from pedestal, goes upstage in disgust, removing costume*) I'm near choked with the stuff out of that can.

PRIEST FIGURE Stop! Stop! Think of your future! (*Rushes back breathlessly into the pulpit*) Let us — proceed — my dear brethren, ah — yes — Matt Talbot — mystic — workman maybe — yes — saint — let us — let us — meditate upon the handiwork of the Almighty.

> WOMAN *gestures back towards the two men. They move up, pushing the trolley between them.* PRIEST FIGURE *intones.*

Let us unveil the remains of the Servant of God (*Clicks fingers*) Hurry up back there!

FIRST MAN I thought t'was to be a sorta trial.

SECOND MAN 'Twas my understanding 'twas to be an entertainment.

FIRST MAN A kind of temptation of the saint.

SECOND MAN A sorta quiz show but without the hand-outs.

PRIEST FIGURE Silence down there!

FIRST MAN How do I look?

SECOND MAN Bloody awful!

FIRST MAN The same to you.

PRIEST FIGURE It's all one in the light of Eternity! Will you get on with it.

FIRST MAN Right! What've we got here on this fine Sunday morning back in 1925 in the morgue of Jervis Street Hospital in the city of Dublin?

He strips the sheet off the trolley. The body is that of a frail old man, bald, with a white moustache. A white towel is about the waist but otherwise it is naked with the torso, arms, shoulders and legs painted garishly with stripes of red and blue.

SECOND MAN Lookit here! Why's it ya always act like a fella that likes his job? 'Tis disgustin' so 'tis the way ya carry on over the corpses.

FIRST MAN Pride, me man.

SECOND MAN Pride? What d'ya mean, pride?

FIRST MAN Our humble job is an art.

SECOND MAN Art me arse!

PRIEST FIGURE What is going on down there?

FIRST MAN Art! We prepare the corpse for its descent and consequent ascent or further descent, as the case may be. Consider the fact that, in an ambiguous sense, our craft is immortal. It's on permanent display in the galleries on the other side.

SECOND MAN Christ Almighty! Here! What'd he die of?

FIRST MAN That's not for us to decide. They decide that upstairs.

SECOND MAN Upstairs? (*Looks up*) Upstairs where? Who's he,

	anyways?
FIRST MAN	(*Busy with papers*) Hmmm. Here we are! June 7th. Ah! Name and address unknown. Age: about sixty. Height: five eight. Approx. Listen to this! Po-lice report (*New 'police' voice*) At about 9.30 a.m. I was called from my post of duty at Parnell Square having pro-ceeded to Granby Lane where I ob-served the deceased on the pathway. There was a priest in attendance —
PRIEST FIGURE	(*Posing*) Yes — yes! Mother Church!
FIRST MAN	Nobody knew the man. I arranged for the ambu-lance from Tara Street and I accompanied the vehicle to Jervis Street Hospital where life was pronounced extinct by Doctor Hannigan, House Surgeon. Signed: Thomas Hanley, Gárda Síochána. That's all.
SECOND MAN	What d'ya mean? That's all?
FIRST MAN	That's all. There's one misspelling. He spells de-ceased 'diseased'. On the other hand, maybe that's what he meant. Policemen survive upon mix-ups in the language.
SECOND MAN	Where's the instructions? Where's the instruc-tions?
FIRST MAN	What instructions?
SECOND MAN	The instructions! If we don't have instructions we can't put a label on him like a normal corpse. If we can't put a label on him we can't shove him in wan of the drawers. It's as plain as day bloody night! God Almighty!
PRIEST FIGURE	Are you ready down there? Time is passing.
SECOND MAN	Oho, time is right! Begod, I'm not going to spend me Sunday cooped up in here waitin' for yer man to produce his papers. No siree! Come three o'clock I'll be beyond in Ringsend for the League match between Bohs and Shels.
FIRST MAN	A soccer match! A soccer match! At a time like this!
SECOND MAN	What's wrong with soccer?
FIRST MAN	Heavens! When we could be on the brink of an apotheosis!
SECOND MAN	Listen here! Tell me wan thing.

FIRST MAN	Anything.
SECOND MAN	All right now. Lave out the dictionary. I'm only asking, y'know. But how's it, how's it, how's it if you're such a fucking know-all about this, that and the other that you end up down here?
FIRST MAN	Down here? We're all down here, so to speak.
SECOND MAN	Down here! Down here! Washin' corpses, cleanin' slops in the mort-u-ary o' Jervo Hospital.
FIRST MAN	(*Pause*) I'm only part-time.
SECOND MAN	Begod, part-time is right.
FIRST MAN	In the light of day I'm an existentialist.
SECOND MAN	A wha'?
FIRST MAN	(*Loudly. Clearly*) Authentic man lives in incessant anticipation of death. Man alone can be properly said to die. Animals merely stop living.
PRIEST FIGURE	(*Hand to ear*) Hark! Hark! Do I hear a soul in torment?
FIRST MAN	(*Hysterical rise*) No one can die for me! I am my own death! It was me dying already in the womb!
SECOND MAN	Don't take it too hard. I wouldn't give it a minnit's thought. Here! D'yis want a fag?
FIRST MAN	(*Towards the figure of* TALBOT) He has assumed the deaths of others. Who does he think he is? Christ?

He approaches the trolley and slaps the face of TALBOT *several times, sharply. Then stands, weeping.*

SECOND MAN	Here! Wha's this? Wha's this? Stop hittin' the corpse. Ya can't be hittin' the corpse.

The WOMAN, *who has put on a lopsided nursing-nun's headgear, comes forward, brightly, carrying chains and cords.*

WOMAN	(*High*) Enter, attractive nursing sister, carrying chains —
SECOND MAN	It's not your turn yet, for Christ sake!

WOMAN *withdraws again, disappointed.*

PRIEST FIGURE Return to the bosom of Mother Church, all you that labour etcetera, etcetera.

> FIRST MAN *rushes towards the pulpit and throws himself down on his knees.*

FIRST MAN Oh, Mother, Mother, I gave it all up when I was fifteen.

PRIEST FIGURE Trust in God's mercy. Let me get down out of here and I'll soon sort you out.

SECOND MAN What's going on around here?

FIRST MAN (*On knees before* PRIEST FIGURE) Oh, Mother, help me over the hump.

PRIEST FIGURE My son, you must trust in Divine Providence, our Blessed Mother Mary, St Patrick our national saint, St Brigid and also several others.

SECOND MAN (*Rooting about under the trolley*) I'm the only one getting on with the job around here. Where's me bucket?

PRIEST FIGURE Now, how long is it since your last confession?

FIRST MAN I feel this may be my last confession.

PRIEST FIGURE Mention everything.

SECOND MAN (*Busy with cleaning*) 'A-roamin' in the gloamin', with my bonnie lass from — '

WOMAN (*Forward, breezily*) Enter attractive nursing sister, carrying chains —

SECOND MAN How's it goin', sister?

WOMAN Men, men, oh men, we're in the presence of a saint! Oh, look what I've got here!

SECOND MAN What've you got there, sister?

WOMAN Chains.

SECOND MAN Chains?

WOMAN And cords.

SECOND MAN Begod.

WOMAN Removed by me at an earlier moment from the body of that holy man lying there before us. One heavy cart chain tightly about the body and hung with numerous holy medals. A lighter chain around one arm, around the other the cord of St Francis, a similar, that is, lighter chain about one leg, around the other, leg that is, a rope tightly tied. He had lived with them for the better part of his life so that the chains, though rusted, had sank into the flesh —

SECOND MAN Mother of Jesus!

WOMAN Oh! Oh! What do you think of that?

SECOND MAN To tell ya nothing but the truth, sister, I think it's kinda peculiar, if ya folla me.

WOMAN I am asking you but you don't have to answer me as I shall answer for you —

SECOND MAN Go 'way!

WOMAN It is — miraculous. Or rather will lead to miracles in time when Mother Church —

PRIEST FIGURE (*Head up*) Yes? Over here! (*Head back down*)

WOMAN — when Mother Church will raise this simple man to the calendar of the saints. One verified miracle is required but others are welcome.

SECOND MAN D'ya mean to say, sister, that that misfortunate little man was carrying around all that hardware on him?

WOMAN (*High*) He is in the company of St Anthony who wrestled for twenty years in the desert with a nightmare circus of demons, St Catherine of Siena whose self-flagellations astounded Satan. From the deserts south of Alexandria to the upper reaches of Cappadocia, across the Spanish plateau and out to the Western rim of our own Irish islands, stylites, anchorites in incredible exercises of penance, chains, poles, hairshirts, beds of nettles, motionless for hours with arms outstretched in the shape of the Cross!

> WOMAN *throws herself upon the trolley and kisses the figure of* TALBOT, *passionately.*

SECOND MAN Hey! Stoppit! Ya can't be kissin' the corpse!

> FIRST MAN *and* PRIEST FIGURE *forward, rapidly.*

FIRST MAN I've made my peace! Hey, everyone! I'm at peace

	with the Lord my saviour! All is forgiven. Good day, sister.
WOMAN	Good morning, Father.
PRIEST FIGURE	Good afternoon, my dear people!
SECOND MAN	Hello, hello! Listen, Father, I've a complaint to make about certain parties here present taking liberties with the corpse. No names mentioned, now.
FIRST MAN	Hey, you! You're sacked. Find yourself something else to do.
SECOND MAN	Sacked! What d'ya mean, sacked?
WOMAN	I noticed he wasn't right, somehow.
SECOND MAN	Listen to me! Yis are all makin' a mock out of the poor corpse. I'm fond of the poor bugger. I has me pride in me work.
FIRST MAN	Work!
PRIEST FIGURE	Work and pray! Let us pray!
SECOND MAN	I mean to say, a body is a body is a body. 'Tis all that's left of him. I knows his kind. Wan of the poor auld hoors offa the streets, sleeping in corners —

> FIRST MAN *has gone back, put on a frock-coat and taken a long pointer and top hat in one hand. He also carries a stethoscope.*

SECOND MAN	Will yis lissen to me!
PRIEST FIGURE WOMAN	}Let us pray. (*They kneel*)
SECOND MAN	Awright! I don't mind the odd prayer. This is different. 'Tis like Duffy's Circus. (*Loudly*) He hasn't anything! So what d'yis want of him? Yis have no claim on him, anymore!

> FIRST MAN *comes and drapes the stethoscope around the neck of* SECOND MAN.

SECOND MAN	What's this? What's this?
FIRST MAN	Just follow the cues, man, just follow the cues.
SECOND MAN	Jaysus, the way they ignore ya!

Both men stand to either side of trolley, facing the audience.

PRIEST FIGURE Let us pray for the Beatification and Canonisation of this holy Dublin working man, that in these troubled times the people might have a model of Christian loyalty and obedience, to fight off the false doctrines, subversive influences, dangerous and foreign practices, that threaten our faith —

WOMAN A-men.

FIRST MAN ⎞ (*Rapping the floor*) Ladies and Gentlemen! We give
SECOND MAN ⎠ you — Matt Talbot! Servant of God!

> *The tableau is held. A church bell rings in the distance, then another and another. Church bells of all kinds in a cacophany.* TALBOT *rises up, painfully. He picks up cords and chains and binds his hands, legs and torso.*

TALBOT (*Slowly, dreamily*) Dear God, I bind meself with the bonds of this earth that I may know the weight of flesh. And learn to free meself from its burden. Mary, Mary, Mother of God, I tie me limbs that I may walk slow and know each step I take and where it takes me to the feet of Christ. St Teresa, help me to silence me tongue, except when it tries to speak to Almighty God.

> *With a sudden, startling energy, he rises on the trolley and flings both arms out in the shape of crucifixion. As he does so, blinding beams of light shoot through the walls of the box, pooling about him and leaving the rest of the stage in darkness. The other four figures cringe back, the women screaming. A high-pitched wailing cry rises, scarcely human but representing human beings in great agony. As it reaches its crescendo it is of physical discomfort to the audience. The four figures race about, hands aloft, to block the lights. Each of the beams is gradually cut off and the sound dies down.*

TALBOT *sinks to the trolley, and kneels upon it.*

FIRST MAN (*Forward, pompous lecture manner, wielding his pointer, addressing the audience*) I find the ah — specimen interesting. Indeed, I was about to begin my autopsy, with the classic incision from beneath the jawbone, here, to the left side of the abdomen, here, when I was prevailed upon by excitable nuns and others, carrying prayer-books, small vessels of water and other items of a religious nature. At any rate. Since the ah — specimen had died of myocardial degeneration I was first of all in pursuit of the heart. You see, my speciality is shock. Shock! What is shock? A difficult term, I agree. Yet there are indications of shock here. No other word for it. Shock, shock. Shock! I have seen the noxious chains by which the specimen bound himself for forty years. I observed the slits in the trousers by which the cloth parted to allow him, without discovery, to kneel on exposed kneecaps, often in the inclement atmosphere for hours at a time outside churches and such like. Absolutely remarkable cutaneous thickness there. The ah — specimen exhibits several indications of prolonged starvation. Or at least curious alimentary habits. But it is difficult to comment on this without extracting chyme or chyle from the digestive tract. Yet, isn't there, how shall I say, a certain proportion to the little fellow? (*Pause. Thought*) Yet there are peculiarities here. Something — odd. If the heart is all, how did it compensate? What effect did such wear and tear have upon its chambers? Did they enlarge? Can we not speculate upon the expenditure of blood? I should have discovered all, if they had allowed me to open the heart! The heart clearly belongs in formaldehyde!

He turns, goes back and is replaced by SECOND MAN *who comes forward, with stethoscope about his neck. When* SECOND MAN *approaches,* TALBOT *begins to move.*

SECOND MAN Sit up, please. Breathe in. Breathe out. Say Aaah.

TALBOT Aaah.

SECOND MAN Ninety-nine. Say ninety-nine.

TALBOT Ninety-nine.

SECOND MAN Cough.

TALBOT Ugh.

SECOND MAN Do you smoke?

TALBOT No, doctor.

SECOND MAN Do you drink? (*No answer*) Do you drink?

TALBOT I did wance, doctor. But never anymore.

SECOND MAN Hmm. That will be all. Get dressed.

> SECOND MAN *walks aside, very professionally.*
> TALBOT *begins to dress — trousers, boots, an old*
> *shirt, frock-coat and derby hat. The* WOMAN *comes*
> *rushing forward, wearing an old black shawl.*

WOMAN Oh, doctor, doctor, what's to become of him?

SECOND MAN Madam, your brother is killing himself.

WOMAN Ah, sure, God help us.

SECOND MAN Sixty-eight years of age, you say?

WOMAN Yes, doctor, the creature.

SECOND MAN Time for a man to put his feet up. Wear slippers.

WOMAN He'll never stop 'till he drops.

SECOND MAN Black fasts, you say?

WOMAN Sure it's only during Lent, doctor, he does the black fast and then in June in honour o' the Sacred Heart o' Jesus 'n also Fridays, nothing at all he takes but the dry bread 'n a wash o' warm cocoa.

SECOND MAN Fridays?

WOMAN 'Twas the day they crucified Our Lord, sir, 'n me brother has it ever on his mind.

SECOND MAN A black fast for the death of Christ?

WOMAN No, sir. For them that crucified him. (*Pause*) He takes a little food of a Tuesday 'n Thursday, maybe an egg or a bitta meat.

SECOND MAN I'm amazed to hear it.

WOMAN Mondays only the black bread and the black tay.

SECOND MAN We've about exhausted the week, I believe.
WOMAN He ates a little dinner on the Sunday, sir, after fastin' through all the Masses.
SECOND MAN Madam, I risk speaking bluntly to you as you appear to be a reasonable woman. The human body, madam, is a machine, madam, albeit the most remarkable device ever constructed. Like every machine it has precise, limited functions. It may be repaired. It certainly needs frequent oil and fuelling. Certain parts respond to greasing, oiling, liquidity. Other parts, like the remarkable Voltaic Dry Battery, cease to function in water. In short, madam, your brother's engine, madam, is deplorably run-down. That will be one guinea, please. Pay my lady assistant on the way out.

> *He goes up with a flourish and the* WOMAN *is left pathetically alone. She turns to watch* TALBOT *who is standing, dazed, by the trolley.*

WOMAN Ye're forgettin' yer hat.
TALBOT Hat? Oh, aye. (*He puts his hat on and begins to move past her*)
WOMAN And where do you think you're goin', Mattie?
TALBOT Goin' to work.
WOMAN Goin' to work! Didn't ya hear what the doctor said of ya?
TALBOT Sister, I hafta go to work.
WOMAN Hafta. Hafta. Always hafta do something.
TALBOT (*Sudden, explosive anger*) Aye, hafta. Always hafta. 'Cause that's what it means to be in the world. We hafta match every minute o' waste with an hour of effort. (*Pause*) I hafta make many hours up. An' there is only today, sister. No tomorrow. Me work makes me see the Eternal in every hour. 'Cause it sickens me. That's work.
WOMAN It's ya want to kill yerself!
TALBOT I'd welcome the dying part. I grant ya that. But that's Gawd's doing, not mine.
WOMAN (*Tearfully*) It's your doing! It's your doing!

TALBOT (*Looking at her in wonder*) Asha, Susan, you don't know what it is.

WOMAN   All I know is I've been trying to keep ya going in wan bit of a room or another, body 'n soul together, since Mammy died, and that's nearly ten years ago.

TALBOT I know, Susan, I know. And I'm grateful to you, Susan, the way you come across to see me regular. Go back, now, sister, to yer own childer. It's near over, anyways.

WOMAN   You were always the same stubborn object, Mattie.

TALBOT Come here a minnit, Susie. Don't be bitter now.

WOMAN   No wan near ya. Brother or sister. Even when we was all small.

TALBOT (*Anguished*) I was marked out!

WOMAN   Ya were no different to anyone else.

TALBOT Everywan's different!

WOMAN   All I remember we was always movin'. Here in Rutland Street. Over to Aldborough near to the barracks. Summerhill, Newcomen Court offa the North Strand, down to Monto, Byrne's Lane offa Potter's Alley, back to Summerhill again, out to Love Lane beyond Ballybough. Sticks o' furniture on top of a handcart, the small wans perishin' with the cauld. Runnin' from the Landlords. But what in the name o' God were we runnin' after? Was it anything better?

TALBOT (*Brusquely*) I don't remind meself of it. 'Tis all dead now.

WOMAN   Mammy 'n us twelve childer. An' auld Charlie me father roarin' 'n cursin' 'n drinkin'.

TALBOT (*Almost to himself*) I pray for his Eternal Peace.

WOMAN   Who?

TALBOT Me father.

WOMAN   He was no worse than another.

TALBOT (*Cry*) He was a great sinner.

WOMAN   Matt, it's our own father you're talking about.

TALBOT I seen him in torments! I seen Charlie Talbot among the damned!

WOMAN   You're very hard, Matt. And hardest on yourself.

TALBOT He marked others.

WOMAN What others?

TALBOT All me brothers. All dead now. It takes another to bring out the worst in everyone.

WOMAN What class of livin' is that? Don't we all need others? Isn't the good 'n the bad mixed in every-wan?

TALBOT If there's any meanin' to the life beyond it's that we'll all be alone in Gawd.

WOMAN Oh, and you're the runner to end us all, Matt. Movin' when the rest of us came to a kinda stop. Wan bit of a room to the next. Drivin' yerself into the ground. God Almighty it's beyond me. Shouldn't we rest in peace?

TALBOT Not in the flesh, Susan.

WOMAN (*Sniff*) Indeed 'n it's easy talk when ya haven't others to care.

TALBOT (*Looks closely at her. Fumbles in a pocket. Holds out his hand*) Forgive me, sister. I'd forgotten. Take this. G'wan. Buy somethin' for the childer.

WOMAN What is it?

TALBOT Only a coupla coppers.

WOMAN I will not. Ya haven't a bit o' bread yerself. I couldn't. (*Shakes her head, looking at his hand*)

TALBOT Go on, Susan. I don't have the need of it. Take it for the childer.

WOMAN I couldn't so I couldn't.

TALBOT Go on now with ya.

She hesitates. She takes the money. She weeps.

WOMAN (*Shrill*) Yer goin' to drop down dead on the street wan day 'n not know it. The doctor said.

TALBOT Maybe so.

WOMAN Will ya do wan thing for me, at least?

TALBOT What's that?

WOMAN Let me pin a bit of paper to the inside of yer coat collar.

TALBOT A bit of paper? What bit of paper?

WOMAN For to say yer name 'n address.

TALBOT What do I need of a name 'n address?

WOMAN Don't we all need a name 'n address?

TALBOT I don't have the need of 'em.

WOMAN Lord save us.

TALBOT Go on home, Susan, to yer own family.

WOMAN Amn't I yer own family?

TALBOT Sure you are 'n yer not, Susie. The way to God was be giving up them that's nearest to me. 'Twas what Our Lord said to the fishermen, y'see. But then I discovered something strange, Susan. (*She begins to move away*) Having given all up, it was all given back to me, but different, y'know what I mean. All the world and the people in the world came back to me in me own room. But everything in place. Nothing twisted 'n broken as it is in this world. Everything straight as a piece of good timber, without warp. (*Looks about. Alone*) Susie! Susie! There's something in me that makes it hard for others to abide me. Even me own. (*Prayer*) Oh, Lord. Help me to prepare myself that I may know my sins. Let Thy light shine upon my darkness! I was cranky with Susan today. Or was it yesterday? No matter. Sometime recent it was. The auld spite risin' up in me again against me own father. When what I was hatin' was the drunkard that was in meself. Who am I to say what good or bad is in another? There was that strange thing in the book I was reading. What was it? About the holy men 'n women who went out into the deserts of Egypt. It says in the book they were waiting for the end of the world. The coming of the New Jerusalem! An' they thought to end the world quicker be taking the vow of virginity. No more little childer! I dunno. I think there's always 'n will be always some sorta urge in humankind to end its breeding. (*Memory*) There was that girl, wance, who talked to me about them things. Lizzie! It was such a long time ago. She used to be in service. In a Protestant rectory she was. An' the priest said I did right. I walked away from her. Ya chose a higher love, Matt, the priest said. (*Upset*) Higher or lower, can ya measure it with a ruler? She said I was going agin me own nature. Isn't it a quare thing the way the body does stand in the way of Eternity? The time will come, says the Lord, when the body, that garment of shame shall be cast off 'n there will be no more male 'n female. (*Pause. Irritation*) That being so, wasn't it a strange thing to make us men 'n women in the first place! Kneel down with ya! (*Kneels*) Bless me, Father, for I have sinned! (*The sound of a thumping heartbeat begins, at first low, then amplified to fill the theatre.* TALBOT *becomes frightened by it. The* PRIEST FIGURE *appears.* TALBOT *is aware of the presence but as if in his mind*) Father — Father — can ya tell me? There's something in me that isn't natural. Can ya tell me what it is, Father? Can ya tell me? (PRIEST FIGURE *disrobes to a bright leotard.* TALBOT *screams and bows his head. A church bell in the distance. He rises*) Hafta go to Mass. Mass! (*Prayer*) With expectation I've waited for the Lord 'n he was attentive to me. An' he heard me prayer 'n he brought me out o' the pit o' misery 'n the mire o' dregs 'n set me foot upon the rock 'n directed me steps. (*Rises. Comes down, pulling on a muffler and hat, rubbing his hands against the cold while the church bell tolls*) Go to Mass, now. Hafta go to Mass. (*He moves forward, kneels, then prostrate, centre stage. Back to audience*)

SECOND MAN (*Forward, to* TALBOT *on cue*) Father, Father, there's a poor man down on the street, here!

WOMAN (*Following, on cue*) Father, come quick, look at the poor creature collapsed!

They prop TALBOT *struggling between them.*

PRIEST FIGURE (*In soutane. Forward. Pious*) My dear people! Do you not know who this is? This is Matt Talbot etcetera, etcetera, etcetera.

Through the following FIRST MAN *goes back, puts on a waistcoat, puts a pencil behind one ear.*

TALBOT	Lave me be. Let me up. Where am I?
PRIEST FIGURE	You poor man! These are the steps outside your church. You were praying before going to work.
SECOND MAN	This is Dublin.
TALBOT	Work? I do not know the day nor the hour.
WOMAN	This is 1892.
SECOND MAN	This is 1913!
PRIEST FIGURE	This is 1977, surely?
SECOND MAN	1913! 1913! The Year o' the Great Strike!
WOMAN	1913. 1913.
TALBOT	Go way outta that 'n lave me alone. I'm well able to walk meself.
WOMAN	Oh, the bad-tempered auld fella!

They leave TALBOT *alone centre stage.* SECOND MAN *walks aside and picks up a timber plank.* WOMAN *and* PRIEST FIGURE *retreat, chatting.*

PRIEST FIGURE	Saints are always difficult, my dear. Not to worry. The church always catches up with them when they're safely dead and buried.
TALBOT	Where's me hat? (*Finds it*) The distractions that are in it! God save us!
SECOND MAN	(*From behind*) Time for work, Matt!
TALBOT	Aye, work. Hafta get ta work.
SECOND MAN	(TALBOT *listening*) Down Gardiner Street, Matt. Cross Beresford Place and out to the North Wall, Matt. Past the stations and Fish Street, Matt, with the early cattle from the markets on their way to the boats. Don't you smell the beasts, Matt? Don't you see the day rising over Ringsend, Matt? Isn't it a great day to be alive, with God in his place over the Custom House?
TALBOT	Me father —
SECOND MAN	Your father. What about your father?
TALBOT	Me father. Oh, me father —
SECOND MAN	Time to move, Matt. Your place is waiting, below in the shed at T & C Martin's. Don't you remember the shed, Matt? The big tomb of a place with the high barred windows away above your head?

TALBOT Me father. (*Eyes up*) May God have mercy on his soul. He was no worse than another.

> TALBOT *turns to* SECOND MAN *who is waiting, holding the length of timber.* TALBOT *wearily removes his coat but leaves on his hat and muffler.* FIRST MAN *observes him intently.*

SECOND MAN Mornin', Matt.
TALBOT Mornin', Mick.
SECOND MAN Grab a hoult of the timber, Matt.
TALBOT Right.

> *They raise the plank to their shoulders and begin to walk about with it in a small circle.* TALBOT *is clearly in great difficulty, breathing heavily.*

SECOND MAN Are ye right, Matt?
TALBOT Aye — aye — right — as — rain.

> TALBOT *staggers.*

SECOND MAN D'yis wanta rest, Matt?
TALBOT No — no — no. No rest.
SECOND MAN No rest for the wicked. Right, Matt?
TALBOT Right.

> *They continue around the same circle.* FIRST MAN *forward, watching them.*

FIRST MAN Morning men. Morning, Dick.
SECOND MAN Mick, sir.
FIRST MAN Eh? Oh. Morning, Mick. How's Matt?
TALBOT Mornin', Mr D.
FIRST MAN (*Aside to* SECOND MAN) A walking saint. Oh, a walking saint. (*Loudly*) Keep moving, men. Keep up the good work.

> *The two continue to circle,* TALBOT *more and more unsteadily.*

Mens sano in corpore sano. Healthy exercise is good for men, men. Don't mind me, men. Keep moving. Many hands make light work, right? The idle mind is the tool of the devil.

TALBOT *staggers, falls on one knee, gets up again.*

I'm proud of ye, men. Best yard in Dublin. No slack. Good bonus for ships catching the tide. Meanwhile, fifteen shillings a week. A just, a Christian wage. The labourer is worthy of his hire. Right, men?

SECOND MAN Right, Mr D.

TALBOT *falls flat. The other two wait impassively until he rises and struggles on.*

FIRST MAN (*More rapidly*) I note yer enthusiasm, men. Loyalty to the firm. Very gratifying, I must say. Hasn't gone unnoticed. Down in me little book. We'll separate the men from the boys on payday, hah? (*New tone*) Pay no heed to agitators, men. This is 1913. Bad times. Law and order threatened on all sides. Not to mention Holy Mother Church. They're everywhere. Could be the man next to you. Say three times every night after yer prayers: Mind the Red under the bed! The good master takes care of his hire. Right? Right. Right is right and left is left. Laborare est orare. Christ carried timber, men. Not a chip on his shoulder. Hah! We're all part of the universal balance sheet. Your bit, my bit, the bosses' bit. All adds up. The world prospers and the devil is idle. In the name of the Father, the Son and the Holy Spirit. Ah-men. (*More wildly*) Cut out the malingerers, mischief-makers, malcontents, evolutionists, revolutionists, libertarians, vegetarians, librarians, historical cyclists, intellectuals, anti-clericals, materialists, rationalists, spiritualists, all kinks, finks, freaks and ambiguous females. (*Loud shout*) Don't break the eleventh commandment!

SECOND MAN Wha's the eleventh commandment, Mr D?

FIRST MAN Thou shalt not.

SECOND MAN Thou shalt not what, Mr D?

FIRST MAN Thou shalt not! Thou shalt not! That's all. No more questions. Look at the time it is! Carry on, men. Keep up the good work.

SECOND MAN Thought there was only ten commandments, Mr D?

FIRST MAN Eleven. Twelve. Even thirteen. Have to add when times get rough. Back to your place. On. Keep it moving. I like your spirit, men.

SECOND MAN What about the workin' man, Mr D?

FIRST MAN What about — ? Can he count beyond ten? (*Uproarious joke*) Ha, ha, hoo-hoo. Can he — can he count beyond — Ho-ho. Oh, Lord! Hee-hee-hee!

SECOND MAN Yer makin' a mock outta the proletariat, Mr D!

FIRST MAN (*Shock*) Stop! I didn't hear that word! Proletariat, bejaysus. Me ears deceive me. This is a Catholic country.

SECOND MAN I don't like it, Mr D.

FIRST MAN I wasn't listenin'. No sir, it passed over me head. (*Abruptly*) No obscenity in this yard. Lookit the holy man there. Every time he hears an obscenity he does another penance. D'yis want to weigh him down with Haily Marys?

SECOND MAN What about the rights o' labour 'n a rightful share in the profits o' production?

FIRST MAN What about me granny? Stoppit! Not another word. Lookit inflation! Keep movin'. Keep up the good work, men. Proletariat, me arse. Another fuckin' word outta ya and ye're out o' me little book. (*Frenzied shout*) Three cheers for the Pope, the Holy Mothers of Ireland and William Martin Murphy, God's appointed employer of the Dublin working class.

> SECOND MAN *stops short.* TALBOT *collapses into a kneeling position, which he holds, the plank falls between them.*

SECOND MAN (*Fist up. Roar*) Strike!

FIRST MAN	Wha's this? Wha's this, now?
SECOND MAN	Strike! This is 1913. I call on every man jack of ye to throw down yer tools. Don't be fooled by false promises. Rise with Jim Connolly. With Jim Larkin 'n the Irish Transport 'n General Workers' Union of Ireland!
FIRST MAN	A Red, begod!
SECOND MAN	On to freedom —
FIRST MAN	A Larkinite!
SECOND MAN	An' the 'stablishment of a Workers' Republic o' the thirty-two counties o' Ireland. North, South, East 'n West. We have nothin'. We've nothin' to lose.
FIRST MAN	Back to yer work!
SECOND MAN	On to revolution.
FIRST MAN	Bejay there'll be no revolution in my yard.
SECOND MAN	(*Selfconsciously*) From the mills o' Belfast 'n the fields o' the West, from the docks 'n desks o' Dublin, from the trams 'n printing houses, we — come —
FIRST MAN	Who come? Where? What?
SECOND MAN	Yis'll hear our feet, marchin'. Wan day, wan day, soon, the people —
FIRST MAN	Now wait a minute, Mickser! What's this people? Aren't we all Irish?
SECOND MAN	There's no nation, comrade, no class, creed nor sexual discrimination, comrade, among the people.
FIRST MAN	Oh, megod, sex now. Don't comrade me, ya ignorant galoot. I'm the foreman. I'm the boss of the boss's orders around here!
SECOND MAN	There's no boss neither, comrade.
FIRST MAN	Bosses there is and bosses there'll always be 'cause some are up and some are down. The law of God and the law of man, me lad.
SECOND MAN	Down with Imperialism! Be men now or be forever slaves. Let a thousand flowers bloom.
FIRST MAN	Flowers? Flowers? Here. (*To* TALBOT) Here. What about him? The saint?
SECOND MAN	What about him?
FIRST MAN	What about him, yourself? Ha?
SECOND MAN	(*Walks over and spits on* TALBOT) Scab! Strike-

breaker!

FIRST MAN Glory be! Spitting on a holy man! Look what you did.

SECOND MAN Where was he in 1913? Down on his knees while the rest of us was tryin' to get up off them.

FIRST MAN Praying!

SECOND MAN Listen, comrade. It all adds up to the wan weight in the scales, prayers and pence, if ye're only counting them for yerself.

FIRST MAN (*Pose*) We have, here, one, who was a model of all Christian workers —

SECOND MAN Go on with ya.

FIRST MAN Another Joseph of Nazareth. Never complained. Did his work!

SECOND MAN Why didn't he take strike pay, so, in 1913? Ha?

FIRST MAN Spent his humble days —

SECOND MAN Why didn't he go on the picket with the men? Answer me that!

FIRST MAN Spent his days — prayin' for the salvation of his immortal soul.

SECOND MAN Prayin'! Listen, comrade, there was a hundred thousand people starvin' in the Dublin tenements. What's the soul of wan man got to do with that? Or vicy versy, the soul of any man has everything to do with that?

FIRST MAN Readin' appropriate religious and pious literature against the evils of the times.

SECOND MAN Jaysus, the way they ignore ya!

FIRST MAN (*Gestures, calls out*) Bring on the books. He needs his books!

> PRIEST FIGURE *rushes forward with armful of books, pamphlets. These are dumped on and about* TALBOT, *who doesn't move, still in a daze.*

PRIEST FIGURE The remarkable library of a simple saint, found after his death. *Socialism* by Rev Robert O'Kane, SJ. Several books by Mr Belloc on the Church and Socialism. Studies of the illustrious Father McKenna, SJ on the workers' problems —

FIRST MAN That will be all, Father. Thank you, the point is made. (PRIEST FIGURE *retreats*) Meanwhile, the Servant of God digested these works of Christian direction and advised his fellow workers on their rightful place in society.

SECOND MAN Aye. Down on their uppers!

FIRST MAN Well, now. That's it. Law and order restored. It didn't work. Consult your history books. Police exonerated. Disturbances exaggerated. The usual protesters. They're all down in me little book. Enemies of Church and State —

SECOND MAN 'Tis only starting!

> *He runs and grabs the flag of the Plough and the Stars. At the same time, the* WOMAN *climbs on to the pedestal in the uniform of Countess Markievicz, wide-brimmed hat with feathers, green jacket and skirt, bandolier and side holster.*

FIRST MAN By Christ, they're off again!

SECOND MAN 'Tis the Countess! The Countess Markievicz herself.

> *He kneels at the foot of the pedestal, flag aloft.*

FIRST MAN Begod we have to do something.

> *He runs to* TALBOT, *waves hands before Talbot's face, generally tries to bring him out of a trance, but without response.*

WOMAN (*Speech*) Let them remember 1913, too, as the year of liberation of Irish women. Sisters, join your men on strike. Our leader too is Larkin. Our teacher, Connolly!

FIRST MAN That's funny. He ought to be saying something. About Christian resignation — or — or — the dangers of the modern world —

WOMAN They have manipulated the Church, manipulated the home, manipulated the family to oppress us —

FIRST MAN He needs more books! Bring on more books!

WOMAN	Oh, sisters, sisters, all that blood of womankind falling like rain through the centuries!
FIRST MAN	Hey, the Countess Markievicz never said that!
SECOND MAN	Into the streets! Up with the barricades!

He and the WOMAN *hold their tableau.* PRIEST FIGURE *forward as before with an armful of books and pamphlets that are heaped on top of* TALBOT.

FIRST MAN	What's up with him?
PRIEST FIGURE	He's praying.
FIRST MAN	Couldn't you get him to say a few words? Off the cuff. Y'know. Dangers of syndicalism. Y'know. Rights of private property.
WOMAN	They will try to clear the streets on Sunday. But Mr Larkin has burned their proclamation —
FIRST MAN	Listen to that!
WOMAN	Let Mr Magistrate Swifte write another of their proclamations. Let the Peelers and the Military line Sackville Street, but Mr Larkin will be there, if alive, and if dead, he's asked us to carry his body in procession.
SECOND MAN	We'll be there, Countess. We'll be there on Sunday.

They resume their tableau.

FIRST MAN	See what I mean? We're in the middle of a revolution.
PRIEST FIGURE	Revolution! Huh! My dear man, shall I tell you why the Church survives revolution?
FIRST MAN	Don't.
PRIEST FIGURE	I shall tell you anyway. It is because the Church is always behind the times and adapts herself accordingly.
FIRST MAN	Tell me that when the economy collapses. What about him? (*Talbot*) It's your job to get something out of him.
PRIEST FIGURE	My job?
FIRST MAN	Look! He could read out of his books. And you give pious commentaries. Or maybe something of his

	experiences of the Great Strike. I was there but I wasn't there. You know what I mean?
PRIEST FIGURE	(*Scandalized*) You mean while he's meditating!
FIRST MAN	Meditating! He's done enough meditating. It's action we want now. The enemies of Church and State are massing in the streets. They're looting the shops and raping convents. Good God, the whole world is dividing into us and them. What use is a saint if he doesn't stand up for us? Good, decent, ordinary, normal, god-fearing, law-abiding, cash-paying customers — I mean people. Who know where their bread and wine, I mean bread and butter, comes from. And what it costs. Why doesn't he do something for the people who are backing him?
PRIEST FIGURE	You talk as if he were a race-horse.
FIRST MAN	Well he is, in a class of a way.
WOMAN	Class!
SECOND MAN	Class!
FIRST MAN	What I mean is, you know, out in front. Into the straight. Setting the pace. Winning post. Winners' enclosure. Short price but a good gamble.
PRIEST FIGURE	Turf Accountancy!
FIRST MAN	The question is. Can he be quoted?
PRIEST FIGURE	That's for the Church to decide, in ah-due ah-course — when this gallant ah-charger, er-ah-mount, no — steed, has reached the ah-winning post.
FIRST MAN	If he's no good alive, what good is he dead?
PRIEST FIGURE	Sanctity! The question is imperative in these troubled times. Our saints — our saints — I mean grace, I mean mediation, between here and there, up there, down here, out there, in here, higher to lower, that to this. I hope I make myself perfectly clear?
FIRST MAN	(*Idea*) Canonisation! You think it'll work?
PRIEST FIGURE	Work?
SECOND MAN	(*Fist up*) Work!
WOMAN	Work! Work!
FIRST MAN	A saint of our own, one of ourselves, begod. That's an idea!

PRIEST FIGURE	Well — not yet — everything in its proper place —
FIRST MAN	(*Breaking up tableau of the others, throwing away flag*) Clear the decks, everyone for the canonisation.
PRIEST FIGURE	No — no —
SECOND MAN	Here, me flag!
PRIEST FIGURE	Death — apostolic enquiry — sacred process —
WOMAN	This is a mockery of womanhood!
PRIEST FIGURE	Collection of evidence — miracles — takes time —
SECOND MAN	Me flag is torn!
FIRST MAN	Where's the Pope?
WOMAN	Sexual repression —
FIRST MAN	No sex —
PRIEST FIGURE	The Church —
WOMAN	Discrimination —
FIRST MAN	Canonisation —
PRIEST FIGURE	(*Finger up*) The Church has her base secure upon the earth but her head is in the clouds — I mean heavens, I mean Heaven —
SECOND MAN	Look!

TALBOT *has risen suddenly to his feet. He stands a moment, swaying.*

TALBOT	(*Great anguished cry*) Oh, Gawd! I seen Satan in the streets! I seen the city like a woman in the dark waiting his coming. I seen the brood of Lucifer in dark uniforms batin' the innocent —
FIRST MAN	Listen!

All five stand, listening. A sound, which grows louder and louder, of thousands of shuffling, marching feet seems to come from some distance. The four figures fall back to the sides in frozen positions. TALBOT *is alone in the centre, pooled in light. The walking feet come nearer and there is pushing, scratching, beating against walls.* TALBOT *moves and touches the walls and there is momentary, absolute silence. Then a great uproar and beating which threatens to demolish the great box. Cries of*

Strike! Strike! *Then great roars of* Larkin! Larkin! *and then above these screams of* The Police! The Police is chargin'! *Sounds of panic, policed attack on bodies and heads.* TALBOT *has thrown himself against the back wall as if holding it with his body. Abrupt silence with* TALBOT *spreadeagled against the wall, back to audience. Lights on the other four in tired postures facing the audience.*

WOMAN (*Tonelessly*) Mr Larkin stepped out on to the balcony of the Imperial Hotel in his clerical disguise. And the people shouted: Larkin! Larkin! We could see him, Casimir, Sydney, Helena and I, from the motor car parked in Prince's Street. Such a crowd! Such a man!

SECOND MAN (*Sunken*) Drunken bastards of police! They were whipped up beforehand like a pack of hounds. Four hundred people in the hospitals. Jimmy Nolan battered to death —

PRIEST FIGURE The people were misled. Agitators, proselytisers, terrorists. There is always a cost to fighting the godless.

FIRST MAN (*Matter of fact*) There's always a Bloody Sunday, a Bloody Friday, somewhere or other. St Petersburg, Dublin, Derry, Santiago. It happens. It passes. Can you name the names of the dead? No. Only the names of places.

WOMAN He was a tool of the Church against the workers!

SECOND MAN He was a scab! He was a scab!

FIRST MAN He was irrelevant!

PRIEST FIGURE He was a saint!

They freeze. TALBOT *slowly moves away from the wall and steps forward. He begins on a low key but gradually rises in power.*

TALBOT (*To audience*) They said to me — 'Tis a strike, Matt. Yis, I says. They said — Ya'll have to take strike pay. For what, says I. For being on strike, they said. I won't take money, says I, for work not done. An' they turned away from me. An' I turned away from them and went to me room. (*Rises*) I seen Satan in the streets! An' I seen it all as wan in Thy sight, O Lord! An' I said to meself:

Blessed be the streets 'n the filth between houses
For they remind us of our failure.
Blessed be the beggar 'n the tramp
For they take the last penny from our pockets.
Blessed be the policeman 'n his stick
For he bates the people outta our anger.
Blessed be the soldiers o' the king
For the hungry wind takes away the smoke o' their
     guns.
Blessed be the body
For its pain is the message o' the spirit.
Blessed be the starvin' peoples of the earth
For they bring down the castles of the mighty.
Blessed be the dung o' the world
For on it is built the City on the Hill!

Slow lights and end of Act One.

ACT TWO

Before the lights go up, the shaking voice of TALBOT *can be heard in the darkness, singing snatches of hymns. The lights find him kneeling on his trolley. To one side, a makeshift tenement kitchen. At a table, drinking their tea, the* WOMAN, FIRST MAN *and* SECOND MAN *dressed, respectively, as mother, little boy and father of the Dublin slums. While* TALBOT *sings the* FATHER *makes rude gestures up at him while the* MOTHER *tries to restrain the* FATHER. *The* LITTLE BOY *giggles to himself.*

TALBOT (*Sings dreamily*) 'Sowl of me Saviour — sanctify me breast — Bod-y of Christ — be thou me savin' guest — '

> PRIEST FIGURE *emerges in pulpit — very old, in soutane and biretta — and prepares to deliver sermon.*

PRIEST FIGURE (*Piously*) Alone, in his little room, his retreat from the world, high above the Dublin tenements, Matt Talbot sings his favourite hymns, beloved of all of us. Below him, around him, the poor of the city, simple good people like yourselves go about their daily lives — Who knows — perhaps touched by that holy voice, raised on their behalf to God Almighty —

TALBOT 'Wash me — waters — streaming from his side — '

SECOND MAN (*Drunken roar*) Will ya shut up outta that, y'auld schemer!

WOMAN Shush! Go drink yer tay.

SECOND MAN Jaysus.

TALBOT (*Sings, shaking voice*) 'To-o Jes-us Heart all burnin' — With fervent lo-ove for men — '

SECOND MAN Shut up! Shut up! Will ya listen to that! I ask yis!

37

	Hymn-singing inside of a house. God Almighty!
WOMAN	Stoppit! Have a bitta respect. Poor Mr Talbot. If ya took example offa him it might do yis good.
SECOND MAN	Him, is it! Is it him? The auld crackpot. Begod if —
PRIEST FIGURE	(*Rapidly*) In this way, the mysterious workings of Divine Grace, passing from saint to sinner. As the centre of Christian life is the Christian family. You may well ask what Matt Talbot has to do with all of this. Although he bound himself to celibacy, although he had foregone the bliss of marriage, the blessing of parenthood, yet he is an example to every father, mother and child amongst us, in his poverty, his obedience, his self-denial, his chastity —
TALBOT	(*Singing*) 'Hail Que-en of Heaven, de O-Ocean Star, Guide of the wanderer, he-re be-low — '
FIRST MAN	(*Little boy voice*) Matt, Matt, the dirty auld scat, Here's a penny to buy a new hat!
SECOND MAN	Shut up outta that, ya little bugger.
WOMAN	Lookit the way ya have the child now.
FIRST MAN	(*Sniff*) Everywan sings that at him.
PRIEST FIGURE	(*Nervously*) I'll ah-leave you with that thought for today, dear mothers and fathers, brothers and sisters. As the modern attacks upon the Christian family close in upon you, divorce — contraception — abortion — drugs — delinquency — foreign periodicals — everything against our Irish way of life — cast your thought upon that simple home which nurtured Matthew Talbot. Draw strength from that sanctuary, that ah-ah —
TALBOT	'Mother o' Christ — Star o' de say. Pra-ay for de wanderer, Pray for me — '
SECOND MAN	(*Jumping up with a roar*) Pray for ya is right! Bejaysus if ya don't stop that caterwaulin' yis'll need yer prayers. (*He picks up things off the table, throwing them wildly; one of the objects flies in the direction of the pulpit.* PRIEST FIGURE *ducks and disappears altogether*) Shut up ya —
WOMAN	Will ya sit still!
SECOND MAN	I won't sit still.

WOMAN What in the name o' God will the neighbours think of us?

SECOND MAN What the shit do I care what they think of us.

WOMAN Oh the dirty language now, in front of the child. Oh that's all yer good for. That 'n drinkin' with yer cronies below on the quays. The way ya go on 'n yer own home.

SECOND MAN Home, she says. Home. Home. Is it — is it — is it this — this rat-hole? Where a man can't have his — his dignity. Where he — he — he can't sit in peace without a racket above and below and parades up and down the stairs of insignificant every sorta riff-raff —

WOMAN (*Cry*) What more can we have with the little we own!

SECOND MAN Own! Own! (*In a fury, sweeping all the dishes off the table*) This — this, is it? Is this what we own?

WOMAN Stop him. Oh, God, stop him with the delph!

She tries to hold him and they struggle. Cries of 'Get off me', 'Don't', 'Please don't'. He begins to beat her, brutally, finally knocking her unconscious onto the floor while he collapses into a chair. FIRST MAN has run forward, petrified, a frightened little boy looking out into the world.

FIRST MAN Me Daddy is batin' me Mammy! Me Daddy is batin' me Mammy! Some of yis come quick! (*Begins to walk back and forth, kicking his feet, looking at the ground*) I know what. I'm goin' off. So I am. I'm goin' on a boat. (*Begins to weep*) Outta this kip. I'll make me way. To Japan maybe. An' when they'll come lookin' for me I'll be gone. Phil! Phil! Where are yis? An' they'll search 'n search. Missin'. I'll be missin'. That'll larn them!

He stops to listen as TALBOT begins to sing again.

TALBOT (*Singing*) 'Sowl of me Saviour — sanctify me breast — Bod-y of Christ — be thou me savin' guest —

39

Blood of me — '
FIRST MAN (*Sudden, lively child's skip. For the first time* TALBOT
becomes gradually aware of him)
Matt, Matt. Where's yer hat?
Yer hair is fallin' out.
The dogs is barkin' at yer feet.
The neighbours talkin'.
The walls is fallin'.
The world is rollin' round.
The sky is darken' overhead.
Matt, Matt, put on yer hat.
The rains is fallin' down.

TALBOT *has climbed down from trolley, slowly,*
dazedly, and gropes forward.

TALBOT Come here, little fella. Come here a minnit to me,
sonny.
FIRST MAN (*From this point on, knowingly 'acting' the part*)
Hello, Matt. (*Pause*) Are yis coming home, Matt?
TALBOT Home?
FIRST MAN Aye, home.
TALBOT Sure I left home, a long ways back.
FIRST MAN (*Mock tears*) The auld fella is batin' me Mammy
again. Rottin' with porter.
TALBOT Here! Here! Wha's yer name?
FIRST MAN (*Knowingly*) Wha's up with ya, Mattie? Amn't I yer
brother, Phil.
TALBOT (*Fear*) No. No. Phil. Phil's dead. All dead.
FIRST MAN Listen to me, Mattie —
TALBOT No. Lave me alone —
FIRST MAN Listen. We could run away from them all.
TALBOT Away —
FIRST MAN Aye. Just the two of us.
TALBOT Hafta get back. Hafta get back to me room.
FIRST MAN We could 'scape. Out to Kingstown, maybe. Or
maybe jump on wan of the trains. Down be
Clarke's Bridge. Where they slow be the Canal.
Jay, 'twould take us anywhere —
TALBOT Anywhere — anywhere —

FIRST MAN Or we could — we could go gatherin' empties in the Quarry offa the North Strand.

TALBOT (*A flicker of recognition*) Empties —

FIRST MAN An' get a few coppers for them — Or get jamjars and catch pinkeens beyond at the Vitriol Works. D'ya remember the big wans, Mattie, swimmin' near Annesley Bridge?

TALBOT (*Tentative, childlike excitement*) Yis.

FIRST MAN Ah, wha's up with yis, Mattie? Yis are always mad to be going places.

TALBOT (*Face lights up. Devilment*) An' we could — 'n we could nip inta Maggie Kavanagh's on the way back —

FIRST MAN Oh, jeepers!

TALBOT An' lift wan of the pigs' cheeks outta the brine barrel when she wasn't lookin' —

FIRST MAN You could be houldin' her in chat 'n I'd lift the mate —

TALBOT An' den she'd start bawlin' 'n we'd be scatterin' down the street —

FIRST MAN It'd be like the time we stole the fiddle off the fiddler. D'ya remember, Matt? God, 'twas gas.

TALBOT The fiddler —

FIRST MAN Auld Charlie, the Da, and the rest of us runnin' down the quays to sell it to the Jewman. We got a few jars out of that fiddle —

TALBOT No —

FIRST MAN An' the auld fiddler bawlin' on the bridge — Where's me fiddle? Where's me fiddle?

TALBOT I tried to find him! I did. I searched for twenty years round all the shelters of the city. Lookin' for him.

FIRST MAN Let's go, Matt. C'mon —

TALBOT No! I had to find him. A wake little dark man. Like an Eyetalian. D'you see him anywhere, Mister? Thought I had him wance. Over in the North Union. Back of the Broadstone. Sure, I knew he was long dead 'n buried in wan o' the paupers' lots. An' what would I've said to him if I'd found him? I couldn't give back to him what we'd stolen offa him. We was young den 'n'd do anything for a drink. We was led, like bastes.

FIRST MAN (*Deliberate*) Hey, hey, Mattie. We could get a drop from the Sailor's pub for a few pence —

TALBOT (*Shock, start*) No, no drink. No.

FIRST MAN Ah, wha's up with ya, Mattie?

TALBOT (*Cry*) It is all — finished —

FIRST MAN Cripes, we'd better get outta here before the auld fella catches us —

TALBOT No. Lave me alone.

SECOND MAN rises out of his chair with a bellow.

SECOND MAN Where's them fuckin' sons of mine?

FIRST MAN Oh, Jays, here he is!

SECOND MAN (*Forward, embracing TALBOT and FIRST MAN, TALBOT shrinking*) Come here, me butties. Is it Mattie and Phil? Well, God bless yis. Me own darlin' boys. What'd I do without yis?

FIRST MAN Hello, Da.

TALBOT (*Trying to break away*) No — no — me mother — Mammy —

SECOND MAN We'll go down now, the three of us, like min, to the corner below, for a few quiet pints, father and sons together, outta this shit-hole. Where'd a man be without his jar 'n the bitta chat with the rest of the lads? Away from the dirt 'n the screechin' 'n bawlin' 'n carry-on of the wimmin 'n childer.

FIRST MAN Right. Da! God, isn't he a caution, the auld lad!

SECOND MAN Right yis are, lads.

TALBOT No — lave me be — no —

The two abandon character and simply drag TALBOT along, to one side, where he collapses to his knees. FIRST MAN holds TALBOT's head back. SECOND MAN takes a bottle of liquor and pours it down his throat, pouring what remains in the bottle over TALBOT's face and clothes. They let him drop and go back themselves to don frock-coats and top hats, each taking a long pointer. TALBOT tries to rise, he staggers drunkenly about, spluttering and retching,

*finally collapsing in a drunken heap. The two men,
as two gentlemen, come forward, poking the bundle
which is* TALBOT *with their pointers. Their exchanges
are cold, sharp, clinical.*

FIRST MAN   Human?
SECOND MAN   Marginally.
FIRST MAN   Young?
SECOND MAN   Difficult to say.
FIRST MAN   Male or female?
SECOND MAN   In the modern sense, both.

They share a short, laconic laugh together.

FIRST MAN   Class?
SECOND MAN   Ah-ah!
FIRST MAN   Artisan.
SECOND MAN   Significant.
FIRST MAN   Indeed.

They share a knowing nod.

Society's burden.
SECOND MAN   One must help where one can.
FIRST MAN   One's duty.
SECOND MAN   Difficult to reform.
FIRST MAN   Their excess. Obsessive.
SECOND MAN   Their lack of hygiene.
FIRST MAN   Their religion.
SECOND MAN   Exactly.
FIRST MAN   Their violence.
SECOND MAN   I was about to say.
FIRST MAN   They wallow.
SECOND MAN   Knowing no better.
FIRST MAN   Deprived of will.
SECOND MAN   Of self-sufficiency.
FIRST MAN   Those old, sturdy qualities.
SECOND MAN   Independence.
FIRST MAN   Responsibility.
SECOND MAN   Rationality.

FIRST MAN	Humanity.
SECOND MAN	That is severe.
FIRST MAN	One has to be —
SECOND MAN	Severe.
FIRST MAN	One has to —
SECOND MAN	Discriminate.
FIRST MAN	One has to —
SECOND MAN	Legislate.
FIRST MAN	Will you begin?
SECOND MAN	After you.
FIRST MAN	No, after you.
SECOND MAN	Please!
FIRST MAN	Thank you.

> FIRST MAN *removes his hat, hat to breast, points pointer at* TALBOT, *head up, addresses audience with a benevolent smile on his face.*

FIRST MAN   Brethren — let us consider — C_2H_5OH — ethyl alcohol. A poison consumed internally by human-kind for thirty thousand years. It is not made, contrary to popular belief, from grape or grain. Instead, these attractive foods are digested by the fermenting germ which, in turn, evacuates alcohol as its waste product. The thought of swallowing the excrement of a living organism is not an aesthe-tic idea. But people will do such things.

SECOND MAN   Indeed.

> FIRST MAN *puts on his hat.* SECOND MAN *doffs his and assumes the position which* FIRST MAN *has just left.*

The addict — dear brethren — is addicted to self-obsession, which is to say self-disgust, which is to say self-destruction. He cannot abide his place on the middle ground. Ascetic and alcoholic are one. Dipsomania and religious mania are two sides of the one coin. Hermit, tobacco and drug-fiend, flagellant and catalyptic visionary, morbid monk and compulsive glutton, masochistic Spaniard on Good Friday. All the same. *Extremists*. True humanity resides in the middle. Society is balance, the enemy is that which is the exceptional. Saints are high, in more senses than one.

FIRST MAN Indeed.

SECOND MAN *puts his hat back on.* FIRST MAN *doffs hat and takes up position as before.*

(*Using* TALBOT *on the ground as a model*) In its passage through the lesser organs, carrying destruction, alcohol finally reaches the higher nerve centres. It dulls the function of the system, takes off the edge, withdraws the film of civilization which thousands of years of evolution have deposited there. It is described as a stimulant. But it is not. That may be how it feels. Not how it is. It is an anaesthetic drug. Drink enough and you fall asleep. Drink too much and you won't wake up.

SECOND MAN Indeed. Keep out the freaks!

Both confronting the audience.

FIRST MAN Keep up the good work!
SECOND MAN It's up to decent people!
FIRST MAN It's down with indecent people!
SECOND MAN Are you polluting your water-supply?
FIRST MAN Are you fiddling the petty-cash?
SECOND MAN Remember! The Golden Mean is *not* a Chinese Restaurant!
FIRST MAN Remember! Hy-Giene is *not* an American greeting!
SECOND MAN Who is this chappie, anyway?
FIRST MAN Will the real Matt Talbot please stand up!
SECOND MAN Please wash your hands before leaving!
FIRST MAN Please wipe that grin off your face!

They go back, chatting.

I think we put it in a nutshell.

SECOND MAN	I was about to say — absolutely.
FIRST MAN	I just adored that bit about masochist monks.
SECOND MAN	Morbid. Morbid monks.
FIRST MAN	Oh yes.

As they go back, the PRIEST FIGURE *comes forward, standing to one side.* TALBOT *crawling, trying to stand, staggering, makes his way in that direction, finally stands, weakly before* PRIEST FIGURE.

PRIEST FIGURE	Young man, I must ask you: Why?
TALBOT	'Tis because — 'tis because I want to give up the drink, Father.
PRIEST FIGURE	But you haven't answered my question: Why?
TALBOT	'Tis because I — I — I hate.
PRIEST FIGURE	And what is it you hate, my son?
TALBOT	I dunno.
PRIEST FIGURE	What do you hate?
TALBOT	I can't give an answer.
PRIEST FIGURE	Oh, that won't do at all. Is it the sin of drunkenness you hate? Is that it?
TALBOT	No — I mane I dunno.
PRIEST FIGURE	You don't know. What's your name?
TALBOT	Me name is Matthew Talbot, Father.
PRIEST FIGURE	And what age are you, Matthew Talbot?
TALBOT	I'm twenty-eight, Father.
PRIEST FIGURE	You're twenty-eight, Matthew Talbot, and you don't know the sin you commit.
TALBOT	(*Flash of anger*) I knows meself!
PRIEST FIGURE	Do you so? Well, maybe it's yourself you hate? The way you defile yourself, the filthy abuse of your own body — ?
TALBOT	(*Who has been shaking his head, in anguish*) No — no — no!
PRIEST FIGURE	Well, Matthew Talbot, I think you'd better go off and don't come back here to take the pledge until you know something more than you know now.
TALBOT	(*Again, flash of anger*) I knows the darkness!
PRIEST FIGURE	(*Pauses. Alert*) Indeed. And where is this darkness?
TALBOT	'Tis in every man, woman 'n child born inta the

world. Most go round, runnin' from it, with fear in der faces but there's no peace till ya walk through it inta some kinda light.

PRIEST FIGURE You're a queer man, Matthew Talbot. Hm. So 'tis to avoid the darkness, so, that you want to give up the drink?

TALBOT (*Impatient*) No — no —

PRIEST FIGURE Well, so?

TALBOT 'Tis because I wanta meet the darkness as meself. I'm niver meself in the drink.

PRIEST FIGURE Well — well — well. Are you practising your religion, at all?

TALBOT Not terrible well, Father.

PRIEST FIGURE We'll have to start there, Matthew. Because there's no change unless God be within you. That's your darkness, Matthew, the absence of God.

TALBOT Beggin' your pardon, Father, I think meself the darkness is Gawd.

A long pause while PRIEST FIGURE *stares at* TALBOT.

PRIEST FIGURE Tell me something. What was it finally sent you here to take the pledge?

TALBOT (*Animation*) I'll tell ya, Father, 'n no lie. We were all offa work, d'ya see, the Daddy, the brothers 'n meself. Not a copper between us. We was outside O'Meara's, y'know, the pub, beyont on the North Strand. Like many's the time before. An' the lads that had the work walked past us into the pub. Nivir askin' us if we'd a tongue on us, y'know. So I walked away. I walked away 'n left me own still standing there agin the pub. 'Cause I saw the emptiness of it all. I saw the emptiness of all friendship in this world. An' I saw meself for the first time 'n I was on me own.

PRIEST FIGURE Hm. It's hardly enough, is it, now?

TALBOT Isn't it enough to know you're on yer own?

PRIEST FIGURE No one is alone, my son, in the community of the Church. We are each in the other and all in Christ.

TALBOT Then I'll be alone with Gawd.

PRIEST FIGURE (*Hesitation*) Well, I'll take a chance on you because I've never come across the like of you, Matthew Talbot.

To each question TALBOT *nods impatiently.*

Are you willing to become reconciled to the teachings of the Church? To obey her commandments? To follow her counsel? To further her mission? To subscribe to her upkeep? To show respect to her ministers? To do all in and through the guidance of the One, True, Holy, Catholic and Apostolic Church? (TALBOT *bows low*) Ego te absolvo — Do you, Matthew Talbot, solemnly swear from this day out, to abstain from all alcoholic drink, in the name of the Sacred Heart of Jesus and in reparation for the sins of drunkenness committed in His sight?

TALBOT I do.

PRIEST FIGURE Go in peace. (TALBOT *stands looking out*) And Matthew Talbot? Pray for me.

> PRIEST FIGURE *walks back.* TALBOT *kneels upon the trolley, his 'bed'. He prays a moment in silence. The* WOMAN *appears, dreamlike, upstage, dressed in hat, coat, a servant girl of the turn of the century.* TALBOT *sits up, aware of a presence, he gradually stands.*

TALBOT Dear Gawd! I bind meself wid the bonds of this earth that I may know the weight o' the flesh; and learn to free meself from its burden.

WOMAN Matt — Matt —

TALBOT Who is that?

WOMAN 'Tis time for me to go back.

TALBOT Go back? Is it Lizzie! Lizzie!

WOMAN Servants must be in before nine, says she. This is a Rectory, not a lodging house, Elizabeth. (*Change*) Our last walk together, Matt.

TALBOT 'Tis so long ago.

WOMAN Well, ya managed to change wan thing for me, anyway.

TALBOT What d'ya mean?

WOMAN From that night out I was never a skivvy again.

TALBOT (*He moves forward*) Where are ya?

WOMAN (*Forward, briskly*) Here I am. We'll have to hurry or the ould bitch will have the skin off my back for being late.

TALBOT I wish — I wish you wouldn't use dem words.

WOMAN Ah — lave me alone, you and yer words. (*Links his arm. They walk*) Isn't it enough to say what ya think? (*Stops again*) I'm not good enough for ya, isn't that it?

TALBOT I never said any such thing.

WOMAN It's written all over yer face for all to see. Just lave me to the door and be done with it —

TALBOT All right, so.

WOMAN All right so! Is that all you can say?

TALBOT What d'ya want me to say?

WOMAN 'Tisn't what I want ya to say. Say what ya have to say yourself.

TALBOT That's what I said, so.

WOMAN God Almighty give me patience with ya!

TALBOT *chuckles and she stares.*

What have ya to be laughing about?

TALBOT I was only thinkin' we're well separated, the two of us.

WOMAN You said a minute ago you were aimin' for something higher. Is it that I'm lower? Is that it?

TALBOT There ya go agin. Twistin' me words.

WOMAN Well, what does it mane if it doesn't mane that?

TALBOT It manes there's something higher than any of us.

WOMAN I used to think — God help us — because you were a good man we'd be happy. It's the other way round.

TALBOT Ye're only bitter, now.

WOMAN Why wouldn't I be bitter? What've we been doing, I ask ya? Walkin' out. 'Less t'was to get married sometime.

TALBOT I never mentioned it. 'Twas you that brought it up.

WOMAN And what were ya doing, so?

TALBOT I was able to talk to ya.

WOMAN You were able to talk to me?

TALBOT Aye.

WOMAN And that's all?

TALBOT 'Tis a lot. For me. I'm not able to talk to too many.

WOMAN *pauses. She is puzzled, hurt, then hurtful.*

WOMAN I think it's all a cod.

TALBOT What's all a cod?

WOMAN All that holy stuff you go on with.

TALBOT Ye're tryin' to vex me. Ya know me bad temper. Don't make me say wrong!

WOMAN Don't make me say wrong! What d'ya think y'are? A saint or something? D'ya think what y'are sayin' is right?

TALBOT Yis.

WOMAN All them promises.

TALBOT Promises? Wha' promises?

WOMAN All that stuff. Peace and rest. Ya said we were going to have it.

TALBOT Everywan can have it.

WOMAN I'm not talking about everywan. I'm talking about us! You and me!

TALBOT Sure ya hafta talk about everywan, girl. And everywan has to have it for hisself. An' if they don't have it for themselves they only abuse oders. Tha's why people in this world do terrible things to oders. They have no quietness in themselves.

WOMAN Well, God forgive you, is that what you think of me?

TALBOT An' I do think that all the sufferin' in the world comes from that 'n all the wars 'n destruction in the world, the terrible hunger for what oders might have, instead of lettin' them be, 'n turnin' to wha's missin' inside hisself.

WOMAN I never abused ya! Never!

TALBOT Asha, ya don't listen to half the things I say.

WOMAN Do you know what I think?

TALBOT Wha'?

WOMAN I think it's afraid y'are.

TALBOT (*Irritated*) Afraid of what?

WOMAN Just — ordinary things. Like getting on with people. That sorta thing.

TALBOT I get on with what I hafta.

WOMAN (*Cry*) Well, what about me so?

TALBOT What about ya?

WOMAN Oh, ya miserable crature — Don't ya see we're only half alive, the two of us? It may suit ya. But begod I want more outta life before they bury me. I want to love someone.

TALBOT I'll go off. I won't bother ya again.

WOMAN Stop. That only makes it worse.

TALBOT I know what you mean. I do. An' I hope — I hope — I hope —

WOMAN I never thought to love anywan 'till I met you. D'ya know I think I must have known from the start. That you'd never be there to love me like that. But instead of stopping me, it drove me on. God help us, women are such fools. The way they love what isn't there. Can ya tell me wan thing? What is it that makes ya go agin yer own nature?

TALBOT But sure I follow me own nature all the time.

WOMAN I give up so — (*Pause*) Mattie —

TALBOT What?

WOMAN D'ya never think of — of having children of yer own? D'ya never think of having a home? I've a bit saved. Not much. But we could get a few rooms. (*No answer*) D'ya never think of them things at all?

TALBOT I think of them day 'n night.

WOMAN Well, why don't you do something, so? Instead of always stuck in that bit of a room. How do you stick it in there?

TALBOT I've measured it. The length and the breadth of it. I fit into it.

WOMAN God, ye're the contrary yoke, so y'are!

TALBOT Yis.

She turns her back on him and unknown to her he
shuffles away into the shadows.

WOMAN   I tauld the mistress inside we were to get married.
Talbot, says she, is he artisan? I couldn't say, Mam,
says I, exactly what he is. He's below in T & C
Martin's, whatever y'd call that. Then d'ya know
what she said? Well, says she, I hope it'll be after
the Horse Show Week. Well, says I to meself, she
can stick her Ballsbridge up under her gansey. And
all her Reverend Mr This and her Sir This, That and
the Other. And her prize begonias. She can raffle
them all off for the Chinese pagans she's so worried
about. By Christ, if there's one thing sure 'n certain
I'll not slave for her again. Does that shock ya?
(*Turns. Finds* TALBOT *gone*) Mattie! Mattie!

> *She stands to one side, head bowed.* TALBOT *has*
> *climbed on to the trolley. He kneels, flings out his*
> *hands as before in the shape of crucifixion. This*
> *time there is no sound, no lights. He drops his hands*
> *limply to his sides and the* WOMAN *goes back.*
> SECOND MAN *comes forward, riding on the shoul-*
> *ders of* FIRST MAN *as a horse, complete with halter*
> *and reins.* SECOND MAN *is dressed in full hunting*
> *gear, peaked cap, riding jacket and boots. They trot*
> *about,* FIRST MAN *neighing, then forward to*
> *audience.*

SECOND MAN   This man must be canonised! We could do with a
saint in the country in these troubled times.
FIRST MAN   Neigh-heh-heh-heh.
SECOND MAN   Religion is in peril. The whole country is in peril!
Look at inflation!
FIRST MAN   Neigh-heh-heh-heh.
SECOND MAN   (*Conversational*) As a matter of fact, just between
ourselves, out at the hunt, the other day — (*To*
'horse') Whoah, there, boy! A couple of us from
Dublin. Some of the Protestant crowd too, but sure
you have to mix with all kinds in these ecumenical

times. There was a time in this country when only a Protestant could get up on a horse. But not any more, I'm telling you, boy. Anyway, what was I saying? (*To 'horse'*) Stand still, you whore, you! Ah, yes. The hunt. There's bloody good connections, by the way, at the hunt. That's not the point, though. There I was. Talking to one of the lads out of the Merchant Banks. No names mentioned, now. Says I, we could do with more like your man, Talbot. Who's he, says he, is he in textiles? Ha-ha-ha-ha. Not at all, says I, Matt Talbot, the workers' saint, says I. There's a man, says I, that was no troublemaker, not like the gang around these days. Begod, Joe, says he, I didn't think you said your prayers unless there was a collapse in the market. Oh, I have my principles, says I, which is the gospel truth, by the way. Anyway, a few of us gathered around on the horses. (*To 'horse'*) Stand still, you bugger. A real mission! Would you believe it? Isn't it mysterious the way God works? I almost cry whenever I think of it! There we were! A group of the most prominent businessmen, and solicitors as well, of Dublin city. The crame of the crame. Sitting on horses out in Enniskerry talking about Matt Talbot, the workmen's saint! Do you know something? Do you know what I'm going to tell you? I'm going to put his picture up, first thing tomorrow, on the factory floor. And another one in the main office. If there was more praying and less marching around with placards we'd soon beat inflation in this country. I'm telling you that, now!

PRIEST FIGURE *appears, reading Breviary.*

PRIEST FIGURE (*Looking up*) Ah! It's yourself, Mr Mac. Taking the air?

SECOND MAN Good-day, Father. Have to get a bit of exercise, y'know. Can't be always working.

PRIEST FIGURE Indeed. It's men like yourself deserve the relaxation.

SECOND MAN I try to do me bit for the country, Father. Not like some. (*Dismounts and leads the 'horse' forward, who takes a close interest in what follows*) Stand away from his head, Father. He might bite.

PRIEST FIGURE Is he dangerous? Tch-tch-tch-tch.

SECOND MAN I was just talking this minute about Matt Talbot.

PRIEST FIGURE Is that a fact? Oh, a good man, Matt.

SECOND MAN Nothing but the best. The salt of the earth. (*With a suspicious glance towards 'horse' who bends to listen*) Tell us, Father. Just between ourselves. (*Loud whisper*) What chance do you think he has beyond in Rome?

PRIEST FIGURE Oh, we're doing our best. We're doing our best. Prayer, Mr Mac. Prayer.

SECOND MAN That'd be the day. A real, certified, Irish saint, at last. That'd settle the mischief-makers, I'm telling ya!

FIRST MAN Neigh-heh-heh-heh-heh-heh.

SECOND MAN *glares at him.*

PRIEST FIGURE I'd better get back to my own prayers, Mr Mac.

SECOND MAN Rightee-o, Father, I'll be off meself. (*To 'horse'*) Come up outta that with ya!

PRIEST FIGURE *has walked down, reading the Breviary. After several attempts, SECOND MAN climbs up on FIRST MAN, turns, and is thrown to great roars and neighs. He chases FIRST MAN back and off. PRIEST FIGURE walks slowly into a spot where TALBOT sits, reading. PRIEST FIGURE looks up and closes the Breviary, slowly.*

TALBOT (*Looking up*) And what do they mane, Father, be the word cat-cat-cat-a-lep-tic?

PRIEST FIGURE (*Standing behind*) It means, Matt, being in a kind of state, in a kind of trance, you might say. Doctors use it.

TALBOT Is that so? (*Chuckle*) When ya think of the words they need!

PRIEST FIGURE If we're to tell others, Matt, we need words.

TALBOT When they came into that room 'n found St Catherine in a corner, prayin', with a white dove on her head, did any of them need words then?

PRIEST FIGURE What's the book you are reading there, Matt?

TALBOT 'Tis about the sickness of the mind. Though the poor man that writ it never knew the Gawd that made him. He has the notion that the holy men of the desert, St Anthony 'n d'other lads, were all lunatics.

PRIEST FIGURE Hm. Pay no heed to it, Matt.

TALBOT Oh, 'tis heed I pay to it, awright. (*Pause*) Sure the man is right but in a way unbeknownst to himself.

PRIEST FIGURE (*Shocked*) What do you mean?

TALBOT (*Testy*) I mane what I say! (*Pause*) If to stay in the world 'n do what the world does is to be right in the mind then the saints was all cracked.

PRIEST FIGURE It's a peculiar way of puttin' it, Matt.

TALBOT It's a peculiar world we're in, Father. What was it St Anthony saw in the cave? Demons? Not t'all. Demons how are yis! He saw the rest o' the world dressed up for a circus. Aye. All the helter-skelter for what it was. Bastes roarin' 'n screechin' 'n rushin' to perdition! There was no demon, only man. An' after twenty years in the cave 'n he climbed out onta the mountain it must have been a terrible relief for the poor fella. Standin'. Lookin' across at the Red Sea in the distance. Like a big cloud on the ground, it says in the book. Gawd knows in his wisdom I'm no Anthony. But I do often have the same feelin' comin' outta this room, outta the house in the mornin'. No wan on the streets but the poor misfortunates that haven't slept. I do often see a light like the beginnin' of the world. But then the auld traffic starts 'n I begin to hurry along, ya know, first a sorta hard walk, y'know, 'n before ya know it I'm in a trot, lathered in sweat, like, runnin'. Aye. (*Slow, sardonic laugh*) Runnin' like a lunatic. (*Pause*) D'ya ever tink, Father, there's any foundation in the notion we

	might be goin' through hell on earth? I do often think so!
PRIEST FIGURE	(*Sententious*) There's a stage when even the holiest of men have doubts. I don't have to tell you. St John of the Cross. Dark night of the soul and so on.
TALBOT	Stoppit, Father — I've me dark night of the soul every time I tries to wash me face in the mornings. Dark night is right! Isn't every other night dark?
PRIEST FIGURE	I'm surprised at you, Matt. It's not seemly. Certainly not. The Church — the Church —
TALBOT	I know the Church is God's house!
PRIEST FIGURE	We're not talking about a building, Matt, but a body of knowledge, teaching — faith.
TALBOT	(*Pause*) I believe, Father, I believe.
PRIEST FIGURE	I'm your friend, Matt. Your friend.
TALBOT	Oh, aye, aye.
PRIEST FIGURE	But this is ridiculous! Someone like you. For years I marvelled at your faith, your devotion. Come on, Matt! Look. In years to come, people will look to your good example, yes, see you as someone to follow in their efforts to —
TALBOT	(*Change*) Don't be sayin' that!
PRIEST FIGURE	Matt —
TALBOT	Don't be sayin' that! (*Anguished tearing at his shirt*) Is it this — this — this ye're talkin' about? The coupla chains round me body. Is that it? What does that make me for anyway? It manes nothin' to anyone. How could it when 'tis only the way for me to know the darkness of me own body. Others are different. D'yis think Gawd wants everywan goin' round with chains?
PRIEST FIGURE	Of course not — I — I —
TALBOT	Would anywan need another to copy if they were able to make themselves inta what they be? If ya'll excuse me, Father, I've no time for the Church devotions when 'tis only people runnin' from themselves.
PRIEST FIGURE	I can't allow you to talk like that, Matt, about the faith of good people, so I can't. No, no.
TALBOT	I knows the people 'n I knows the streets. It's a

distraction from misery most peoples want in a church, small blame to them.

PRIEST FIGURE But what about your own devotion to — to St Teresa and St Catherine —

TALBOT Aye, aye. They're a grand coupla girls so they are.

PRIEST FIGURE (*Uncertain*) Hm. Yes — yes.

TALBOT Ya have to stand alone forninst yer maker. Every-wan has to do this hisself. After that there's no company in this life from saint nor sinner.

PRIEST FIGURE But that's pride, man!

TALBOT (*Innocently*) I do often pray against pride, Father.

PRIEST FIGURE (*Long pause*) What do you see, Matt?

TALBOT What do I see?

PRIEST FIGURE Yes.

TALBOT I dunno what ya mane, Father.

PRIEST FIGURE Well, I never asked you this before, Matt. I respect the privacy of the soul, I do, I do. But — well, when you pray — when you kneel for hours with arms outstretched, Matt, you must see — you must gain the presence —

TALBOT (*Brusquely*) Nuthin'.

PRIEST FIGURE Nothing!

TALBOT Nuthin'! Nuthin'! Nuthin'!

PRIEST FIGURE You mean — you mean you — remove yourself?

TALBOT Oh, I'm there right enough. (*Aggrieved*) Why d'ya ask me? I can't say.

PRIEST FIGURE I understand, Matt, I understand. You simply place before you some picture of the throne of God, some figures of the heavenly host, some —

TALBOT Arragh, Father, stoppit! (*Pause*) Maybe in the beginning I seen them all, up in the clouds, but sure that's only like pictures in the prayer book. 'Twas the dream o' the child in me. Or maybe that's the only way ya can think about them things or talk about them. (*Annoyance*) Sure Gawd Almighty isn't puttin' on a show in the picture palace!

PRIEST FIGURE (*Lost. Sermonizing*) We place before us in our mind's eye an image of holy worship. We concentrate ourselves upon it, removing ourselves from the world about us. In this way we come to —

TALBOT (*Sudden outburst. Very high sing-song intonation*) Gawd is wan! In the world everything's more than wan. We die to become wan again 'n there be no numbers to count beyond the grave. There be nuthin' to see when Gawd comes 'cause there's nuthin' other than yerself 'cause yerself is wan with what ya see so ya see nuthin' 'cause ya can only see what's separate than yerself, ya can only count what's different, not the same, not the wan, the only —

TALBOT *slumps, exhausted.* PRIEST FIGURE *comes right up behind him.*

PRIEST FIGURE Matt! Matt!
TALBOT Whassit?
PRIEST FIGURE Matt!
TALBOT Aye. Aye.
PRIEST FIGURE What is it you wanted, Matt?
TALBOT (*Shakes his head a few times. Face lights at memory*) To tell yis the truth, I never wanted anything but to work wid timber —
PRIEST FIGURE Timber?
TALBOT Aye. Timber. I used to walk round 'n round the sheds when the fresh lumber used to come off the boats. Piles 'n piles to the roof. An' I'd run me hand along the grain. An' I'd fill me smell with the sap. Long ways away they came from where there's big woods. An' I'd see the trees 'cause timber never dies when 'tis cut, only changin' with age.
PRIEST FIGURE (*Slowly, in a whisper*) And what do you want of me, Matt Talbot?
TALBOT An' who are you?

Behind him PRIEST FIGURE *disrobes to an* OLD WOMAN, *long dress, long grey hair. She places her hands on* TALBOT's *shoulders, gently rocking him from side to side.* TALBOT *closes his eyes and rocks silently for a little while. The sound of a thumping heartbeat begins again.*

Oh, Mother! Mother! Mother! Oh, Mother of God! (*As the thumping sound dies away* TALBOT *is left alone, in light. He manages to get to his feet and put on his hat*) 'Tis time. 'Tis mornin'. (*A church bell in the distance. He raises his head*) Oh, Gawd, let the sun come up. (*Chanting voice*) With exception I've waited for the Lord 'n he was attentive to me. An' he heard me prayers 'n he brought me outta the pit o' misery 'n the mire o' dregs. An' set me feet on a rock 'n directed me steps.

> *He comes forward, unsteadily, to one side of the stage, blinking, pulling the muffler around his neck, rubbing his hands and shivering with the cold.*

Hafta go to Mass before work. Hafta go to work soon. Hafta go —

> *Lights up on* FIRST MAN *in the pulpit, holding a loud-hailer and wearing a football supporter's paper hat.*

FIRST MAN (*Very rapid commentary*) Yes! Ladies and Gentlemen, at great expense to the management we give you the greatest athletical — theological — metaphysical performance of all time! (*More church bells begin to peal out, now near, now far*) Yes! Ladies and Gentlemen. Five a.m. the morning of whatever morning it was for forty, yes forty years —

> *His commentary follows the actions of* TALBOT. *When* TALBOT *hears a church bell he sets off across the front of the stage in an odd, loping half-run, half-walk. Reaching the far side he sinks down to his knees praying. Another church bell, again he raises his head, rises, sets off back again across the stage as before, but more painfully. Reaching the other side he drops to his knees once more, praying. Again a church bell. This third time he makes the journey under severe stress, staggering, and is at*

59

centre stage when he collapses, prostrate. The effort should be of a gradually weakening animal in a cage.

FIRST MAN He's off! He's out! He's up! He's down! He's up again! What a man! He's there! The Jesuits in Gardiner Street. He's in! (TALBOT *kneels*) He's down! First Mass of the day! With the rest of us in bed. What a man! Mass over. (TALBOT *off again*) Just look at that pace, that stamina! Pell-mell down Sackville Street, as it was then known. Over the bridge! On to the Carmelites in Clarendon Street. (TALBOT *on his knees*) He's down, folks — Two Masses up. One to go! Not a dint in his determination. What a body action! (TALBOT *moves again*) He's up! He's off! (*High rising note*) Jumping over trolley cars, crawling over banks, scrambling over warehouses! Surmounting what is commonly called material reality! Swinging out of steeples and — and — He's there, yes, there! He's made it! (TALBOT *prostrate centre stage*) There! Prostrated before Adam and Eve's down on the quays. I make it, yes, make it, three Masses plus numerous ejaculations, meditations, exercises of a religious nature en route, yes, in under one hour and forty-three minutes — just inside the record, folks, consult your street maps, put geography against philosophy and work it out! Nothing in his demeanour to attract attention. Nothing out of the ordinary but the short gallop. A simple, ordinary man, you might say, just like you and me, just going about, minding his own transcendental business. (*Pause, change*) No signs of the hidden chains. Dragging him down. Dragging him down. (*Stop. Loud scream*) Oh, Adam! (*Pause*) Oh, Eve! (*Pause*) Quid fecisti? (*Very low*) All this for that. (*Sudden change again. Loud annoyance. Standing up on the pulpit*) There's a smell in here! A stench! (WOMAN *and* SECOND MAN *come forward noisily calling*) A smell? Where? I don't get it, do you?

	(SECOND MAN *is dressed in rough work-clothes.* WOMAN *wears a black shawl.* SECOND MAN *produces aerosol can and sprays all about.* WOMAN *walks about sniffing*) Yes, but, a smell? (*They deliberately step back and forth across the body of* TALBOT)
FIRST MAN	(*Pointing to* TALBOT) Can't you see, can't you, that it's him!
WOMAN	Who? Him?
SECOND MAN	I'd never've believed it.
FIRST MAN	It's — it's his — his body.
WOMAN	Well, I never! Body odour!
SECOND MAN	So that's it!
FIRST MAN	It's how he — smells himself. It's how he — wishes to smell. It's how he wishes — to be.
WOMAN	Oh, course.
SECOND MAN	It's disgustin', so 'tis.
WOMAN	Some people!
SECOND MAN	I get it now. (*Sniffs*)
WOMAN	A bit like — perspiration. (*Sniffs*)
SECOND MAN	Sweat. (*Sniffs*) Definitely sweat.
WOMAN	It's like — must.
FIRST MAN	It's like dust.
WOMAN	Dying.
FIRST MAN	Ordure.
SECOND MAN	Shit. Def'ney shit.
FIRST MAN	(*Scream*) Can't you see, can't you, that he defiles us! Don't you understand that he put himself in our place? That he assumes us in himself? That he would reduce us to his — his — smell?
WOMAN	The nerve!
SECOND MAN	That yoke!

> FIRST MAN *descends pulpit and walks forward to join them over* TALBOT.

FIRST MAN	We are all normal.
WOMAN	Course.
SECOND MAN	Never felt normaller in me life.
WOMAN	Should I get my hair cut?
SECOND MAN	How's your mother doing?

FIRST MAN	Sanitation.
WOMAN	Beautification.
SECOND MAN	Conversation!
FIRST MAN	Canonisation!
WOMAN	D'you like me hair up or down?
SECOND MAN	(*Head up*) D'yis think it'll rain? Maybe a drizzle. A drop.
FIRST MAN	Please! Stop it! He threatens our freedom.
WOMAN	Free? Sure, I'm free.
SECOND MAN	I never felt freer in me life.
FIRST MAN	Glory be to me on the highest! I think, I talk, I feel, I belch, I breed, I faint, I fall, I rise! Therefore I am I. (*Points to others*) You are you. We are not we. (*Points triumphantly at* TALBOT) Therefore, he cannot be us! (*With a roar. Hands up*) God is Man!
SECOND MAN	(*Outrage*) God is God!
WOMAN	God is Woman!
SECOND MAN	God Almighty!

> TALBOT *suddenly springs to his feet. The others cringe away from him.*

TALBOT	(*Flinging out his arms*) Get thee behind me, Satan. (*Pauses, gasping, then quietly*) They said: Lave him alone. Sure it's only Matt. Sure what'd he know about anything? Sure he's not in this world at all. (*Memory*) An' all those years I seen the world made right and straight in me own room. Was it dreaming I was? With them terrible things still going on in the streets. Oh, Gawd, will it ever change in this world? (*Cry*) Christ let out! Haven't I been yer auld fool long enough? (*Change*) God forgive me! It's afraid o' the last darkness I am. When I should see it as the start of Eternal Light. There is a little distance left to me to go. (*Gesturing back to the other figures*) Leave me! Leave me to go it alone! Leave me!

> The two MEN *and the* WOMAN *slink through openings of the box, leaving it altogether.* TALBOT

staggers forward and kneels. The PRIEST FIGURE *has come down behind him, a grotesque old crone, attending but rigid.*

A very little while and all will be over with thee here. See how it stands with thee in the next life. Man today is, 'n tomorrow he is seen no more. An' when he is take out of sight, he is quickly also out of mind. Hafta — hafta go to —

He tries to rise but falls back into a lying position, supporting himself on one elbow. From distress he changes to a mood of childlike reverie.

The old man worked at the bench, shavin' the yella timbers in the sunlight. An' the boy used help him. They worked together. They niver spoke. No need for words. Nuthin' was heard but the sound of timber. Then wan day — wan day, the boy left. He put down the tools outta his hands. Again, nare a word. The old man came to the door with him. They kissed wan another. Then the mother came like a shadda from the house 'n she kissed the boy too. Then the boy walked down the road in the dust 'n the hot sun. An' way in the far distance of the city he could hear them, the sound of the hammers 'n they batin' the timbers inta the shape o' the cross.

A single, distant church bell. The great doors of the box are closed from without by the two MEN *and the* WOMAN *who stand looking in through cracks in the walls from which bright light comes which illuminates their faces.*